The Lunch B

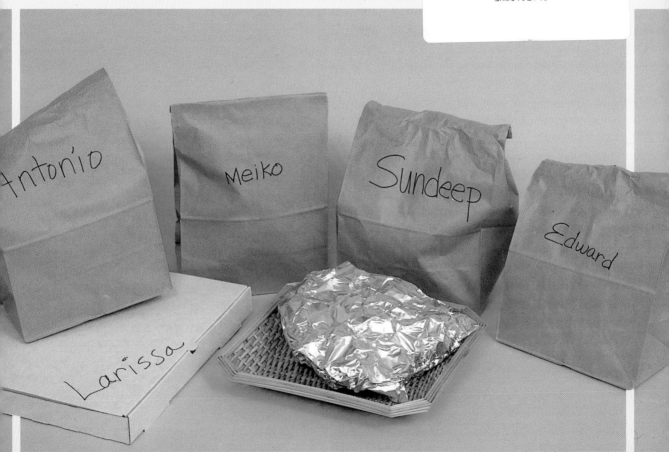

We are
the Lunch Bunch.
We like to bring
food to school
to share.

Meiko brought
sushi for lunch.

3

Sundeep brought
chicken curry
and chapattis
for lunch.

Sundeep's family
is from India.

India

A chapatti is
a kind of flat,
round bread.
It is baked in
a clay oven called
a tandoor.

Antonio brought
tostadas for lunch.

11

Antonio's family
is from Mexico.

Mexico

Tostadas are made
with toasted
corn tortillas.
They have beans,
chicken, lettuce,
cheese, sour cream,
and salsa on top.

Larissa brought
pizza for lunch.

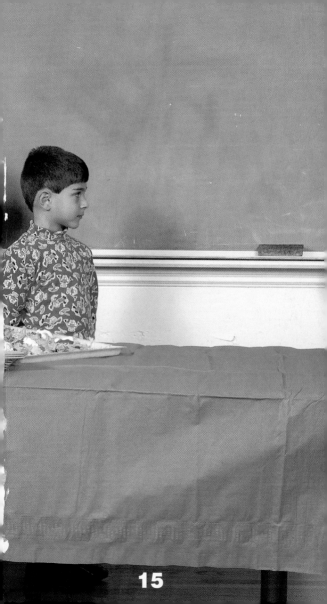

Larissa's family
is from Italy.

Italy

Pizza dough
is rolled into a
flat, round shape.
Sometimes people
throw it in the air
to stretch it out.

Edward brought
fortune cookies
for lunch.

19

Our shared lunch
smells good.
Our shared lunch
looks good.

Our shared lunch
tastes good, too!

24